R.L. 4.1
PTS 0.5

Aunt Harriet's Underground Railroad in the Sky

Aunt Harriet's Underground

Railroad in the Sky

FAITH RINGGOLD

Crown Publishers, Inc. · New York

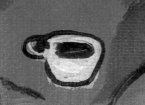

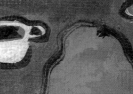

This book is dedicated to my big sister, Barbara Knight. She was never afraid of anything. She is no longer alive, but her spirit is. Barbara would have taken a ride on Aunt Harriet's Underground Railroad in the Sky, and I would have followed her blindly, in mortal fear of going home without her.

Thanks to my daughter Barbara Wallace for the research on Harriet Tubman that appears in this book. And to Janet Schulman, my publisher at Crown, for suggesting Harriet Tubman as the subject for a second book. It is just exactly what I wanted to do. And to Simon Boughton, my editor, for believing it could fly.

Library of Congress Cataloging-in-Publication Data
Ringgold, Faith
  Aunt Harriet's underground railroad in the sky / Faith Ringgold.
    p. cm.
  Summary: With Harriet Tubman as her guide, Cassie retraces the steps escaping slaves took on the Underground Railroad in order to reunite with her younger brother.
    1. Tubman, Harriet, 1820?–1913—Juvenile fiction.   2. Underground railroad—Juvenile fiction.   [1. Tubman, Harriet, 1820?–1913—Fiction.   2. Underground railroad—Fiction.   3. Brothers and sisters—Fiction.   4. Afro-Americans—Fiction.]   I. Title.   PZ7.R4726Au   1993   [E]—dc20   92-20072
  ISBN 0-517-58767-X (trade)
    0-517-58768-8 (lib. bdg.)   10 9 8 7 6 5 4 3 2 1   First edition

One day, my baby brother Be Be and I were flying among the stars, way way up, so far up the mountains looked like pieces of rock candy and the oceans like tiny cups of tea. We came across an old ramshackled train in the sky.

A tiny woman in a conductor's uniform appeared on the steps of the train and announced the schedule:

"All aboard! All aboard! Maryland, Delaware, Pennsylvania, New Jersey, New York, Niagara Falls, Canada. All aboard! All aboard!"

Hundreds of bedraggled men, women, and children filled the sky and boarded the dusty old wooden train. No one spoke. It was like watching a silent movie.

"Come on, Cassie," Be Be said, jumping up on the train. "Let's take a ride."

"Get off that train, Be Be! I'll tell Mommy and Daddy, and you will be in a world of trouble," I yelled.

But the train quickly moved off through the sky and disappeared. All I could see now were flashing lights, sending a threatening message through a sea of clouds:

GO FREE NORTH OR DIE! GO FREE NORTH OR DIE! GO FREE NORTH OR DIE!

"Be Be, come back! Mommy and Daddy will never forgive me for letting you go!" I screamed. Then the woman conductor's voice came like a soft whisper in my ear:

"Hello, Cassie. I am Harriet Tubman. People call me Aunt Harriet because I take care of them. During slavery, I carried hundreds of men, women, and children to freedom on the Underground Railroad, and never lost a passenger.

CAPTAIN BONDAGE

"Let me tell you about slavery, Cassie," Aunt Harriet said. "We were brought here from Africa, as slaves, to work long hours on plantations for no pay. More of us died on the ships coming over than ever reached these shores.

"If we tried to escape and were caught, we might have a foot cut off or get sold away from our families. And then we never saw our families and friends again.

"A legal or church marriage was not allowed. So instead a man and woman would jump the broom.

"It was against the law for a slave to learn to read or write.

"Or have a meeting, even to preach the word of God.

"Every one hundred years that old train will follow the same route I traveled on the Underground Railroad so that we will never forget the cost of freedom. Sometimes the train is a farmer's wagon. Sometimes it is a hearse covered with flowers—inside, a live slave hides in a coffin. You missed this train, Cassie. But you can follow, always one stop behind. When we reach freedom in Canada, you will be reunited with Be Be.

"Cassie, though you can fly, being a slave will suck you to the ground like quicksand. You will have to walk many miles through the woods and waters on blistered feet. And there will be bounty hunters eager to collect the reward on your head.

"Follow the North Star. In daylight, look for moss growing on the side of the tree that faces north. Along the way, there will be Underground Railroad agents to give you a place to stay, clean clothes, and food. But until you reach Canada, you are not safe. Go and don't turn back! And remember: If you are caught, you will be severely punished.

"Follow the river north until you reach a clapboard house with green shutters and
a red-brick chimney. There will be a blind railroad agent who will ask you to sing a song.
You will sing 'Go down, Moses—way down in Egypt land! Tell ole Pharaoh, Let my people
go!' She will give you food and a place to sleep. By nightfall, you must be on your way
through the woods."

I found Be Be's baseball cap floating in a swamp. It was worn to shreds. I squeezed the mud out of it.

"Leave the cap, Cassie!" Aunt Harriet's whispering voice said. "Go on to a weather-beaten frame house with a star quilt flung on the roof. If you don't see the quilt, hide in the woods until it appears. Then it is safe to go in. The next night, follow the road to the bridge, several miles away."

I traveled through the woods and swamps. I was cold, wet, and very hungry. But I could not turn back. When I reached the bridge, I hid in a graveyard on a hill overlooking the river. It was there I found Be Be's toy soldiers and a set of his baseball cards buried alongside the grave of a boy Be Be's age. I was too afraid to cry. I lay awake till I heard Aunt Harriet's familiar whisper:

"Wait for a railroad agent disguised as a gravedigger. He will say: 'I bring you a ticket for the railroad.'"

Now the tears came streaming down my cheeks like rain. I would see Be Be soon... soon...soon.

In a tiny yellow house on the edge of the city, a little girl my age gave me a ticket for the steam car and sewed a fake Pass to Freedom she had made on my undershirt. It read: CASSIE LOUISE LIGHTFOOT, FREE-BORN IN NEW YORK.

"Show that to anyone who tries to take you back to the slaves' plantation," she said.

I reached the back door of a shoemaker's house and knocked three times. That time I slept in a secret room behind a bookcase. Be Be had been there and left another note.

Dear Cassie, I have a new baby sister. She was born today.
Her name is Freedom. Her mother got sick and went to heaven.
She let me carry Baby Freedom on my back. Love, Be Be

After a few days' rest, I started out again, with new shoes the shoemaker made me.
"Move on, Cassie," Aunt Harriet's voice told me. "You are very close to the border of the free state of Pennsylvania. Look for the letter P written on a rock facing north. But still beware of bounty hunters. They can kidnap you at any time. Until you reach Canada, you are not safe."

In New York, a bookbinder hid me in a secret compartment he had built into his wagon. In a downpour of rain, he delivered me to a funeral parlor. There was a funeral going on, so no one noticed me. The undertaker gave me a withered rose Be Be had left, pressed in a book, with a note.

Dear Cassie, We stayed at the house of a millionaire.
He gave Aunt Harriet a bunch of money. We will never
be hungry again. Love, Be Be

The undertaker gave me a fresh-cut rose, hid me in a coffin in his hearse, and took me to Niagara Falls. Now I was just over the bridge from Canada.

I could see Aunt Harriet and Be Be, with Baby Freedom still tied to his back, the passengers on the Underground Railroad, and women all dressed in white flying in a huge circle around them.

"We're free! We have shook the lion's paw!" Aunt Harriet yelled in a voice that shot through the air like a joyous bolt of lightning.

"Go down, Moses!" Be Be said.

"And let my people go!" the others sang out.

I kissed Be Be over and over, and I made him promise he'd never, ever leave me again.

"I love you, Cassie, but I had to go," Be Be said. "Freedom is more important than just staying together, and what's more, I got to ride on the Underground Railroad with Harriet Tubman. Now I know what our great-great-grandparents survived when they were children."

CELEBRATING
1849 · 1949
100 TH
ANNIVERSARY
UNDERGROUND
RAILROAD

That day there was a big feast, and a quilt celebrating the one hundredth anniversary of Harriet Tubman's first flight to freedom hung in the sky. People came to eat, dance, and sing praise to Aunt Harriet—for taking us from slavery to freedom and for being the Moses of her people.

Harriet Tubman was born a slave in about 1820 in Bucktown, Maryland. Her father taught her to hunt, swim, imitate bird calls, and survive in the woods. Her mother taught her nursing skills and how to use herbs for medicine. Though Harriet could neither read nor write, with these survival skills she escorted over 300 slaves to freedom on 19 trips on the Underground Railroad—without ever losing a passenger. Among them were her aged mother and father and all her brothers and sisters.

The Underground Railroad was a network of people and hiding places. The first accounts of slaves escaping on the Underground Railroad date from as far back as 1787. Harriet Tubman's own escape north was made in 1849, with the help of a Quaker woman whom she encountered on the road near the plantation fields. The woman directed Harriet to the house of a German farmer and his wife. With their assistance, and that of many other "conductors," Harriet reached freedom in Canada. She returned to become a conductor herself, guiding groups of slaves north through Pennsylvania, New Jersey, and New York to Canada, where the government refused to return former slaves to their American masters. She traveled mainly at night, sang songs as signals to other people, and carried a pistol to defend herself. Slave traders placed bounties ranging from $10,000 to $40,000 on Harriet's head.

As a young girl, Harriet was gravely injured when she was struck by a weight thrown by a slave master.

The injury left her marked for life and caused her to have frequent blackouts, which could last anywhere from a few seconds to several hours. This strange malady persisted throughout her life but never diminished her courage or impeded her victorious flights to freedom.

While ill and near death, she had strange dreams of flying to freedom, with the aid of a circle of ladies dressed in white. In *Aunt Harriet's Underground Railroad in the Sky,* I used this dream, as well as the slave custom of throwing a quilt over the roof of a house for good luck, for its visual clarity. The route by which Harriet Tubman took her passengers to freedom forms the structure of the book. I used some of the actual stops, or "stations," though not the exact persons or conductors.

The real conductors were white sympathizers, free-born Negroes, and escaped slaves, many of whom were women. They embraced every religion, and none. Some important conductors were John Fairfield, who belonged to a Virginia slaveholding family and who posed as a slave trader; the Quaker Thomas Garrett, who ran a station in Wilmington, Delaware, known for comfort for all who could reach it; William Still, a coal merchant, free-born in Pennsylvania; Gerrit Smith, in New York, a millionaire philanthropist; Stephen Myers, a Negro book publisher who kept records of escaped slaves; and the Reverend J. W. Loguen, himself an escaped slave. On the western escape route that went through Cincinnati, Ohio, Levi Coffin, a Quaker, helped more than 3,000 slaves to freedom. When runaways got as near to the border as Rochester, New York, Susan B. Anthony and Frederick Douglass (also a runaway slave, in 1838) assisted them in making the last jump into Canada, called the "Promised Land" by some slaves.

During the Civil War, Harriet Tubman served as a nurse, a spy, and a commander of intelligence operations in the Union Army. She was unique in that she commanded forces of men both black and white and was never captured. Nonetheless, she was denied a war pension, although she did receive a war widow's pension when her husband, Nelson Davis, died in 1888.

Harriet's autobiography, *Scenes in the Life of Harriet Tubman,* was dictated to Sarah Bradford and published in 1869. A revised edition was published under the title *Harriet: The Moses of Her People* in 1886. Harriet's door was always open to those in need. She died on March 10, 1913, in Auburn, New York. She was given a full military funeral.

—Faith Ringgold

Further Reading

Sarah Hopkins Bradford, *Scenes in the Life of Harriet Tubman* (Auburn, New York: W. J. Moses, 1869)

Sarah Hopkins Bradford, *Harriet: The Moses of Her People* (New York: J. J. Little & Co., 1886)

Charles L. Blockson, "The Underground Railroad" (*National Geographic,* July 1984)

Judy Carlson, *Harriet Tubman: Call to Freedom* (New York: Fawcett Columbine, 1989)

Kate McMullan, *The Story of Harriet Tubman, Conductor of the Underground Railroad* (New York: Dell Publishing, 1991)

Ann L. Petry, *Harriet Tubman: Conductor on the Underground Railroad* (New York: Crowell, 1955)

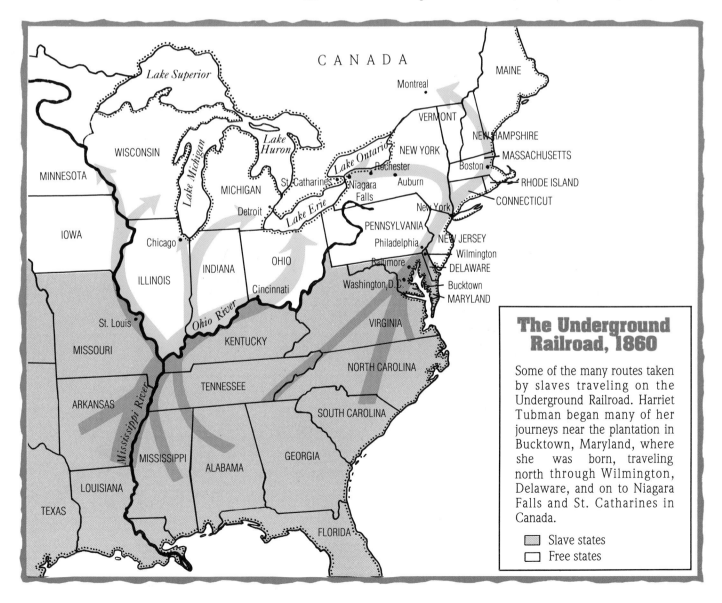

The Underground Railroad, 1860

Some of the many routes taken by slaves traveling on the Underground Railroad. Harriet Tubman began many of her journeys near the plantation in Bucktown, Maryland, where she was born, traveling north through Wilmington, Delaware, and on to Niagara Falls and St. Catharines in Canada.

▨ Slave states
☐ Free states